JOHN THOMPSON'S
EASIEST PIANO COURSE

FIRST SMASH HITS

Arranged by Christopher Hussey

Teachers and Parents

This collection of pop songs, arranged in the John Thompson tradition, is intended as supplementary material for advancing young pianists in the Easiest Piano Course or other similar methods. Listed in the suggested order of study, most students can begin playing the simpler arrangements after Part 1, and the difficulty level progresses through to Parts 3 and 4. The pieces may also be used for sight-reading practice by more advanced students.

ISBN 978-1-70513-176-3

WILLIS MUSIC

EXCLUSIVELY DISTRIBUTED BY
HAL•LEONARD®

T0057217

Visit Hal Leonard Online at
www.halleonard.com

Contact us:
Hal Leonard
7777 West Bluemound Road
Milwaukee, WI 53213
Email: info@halleonard.com

In Europe, contact:
Hal Leonard Europe Limited
42 Wigmore Street
Marylebone, London, W1U 2RN
Email: info@halleonardeurope.com

In Australia, contact:
Hal Leonard Australia Pty. Ltd.
4 Lentara Court
Cheltenham, Victoria, 3192 Australia
Email: info@halleonard.com.au

All Is Found

from FROZEN 2

Music and Lyrics by Kristen Anderson-Lopez
and Robert Lopez

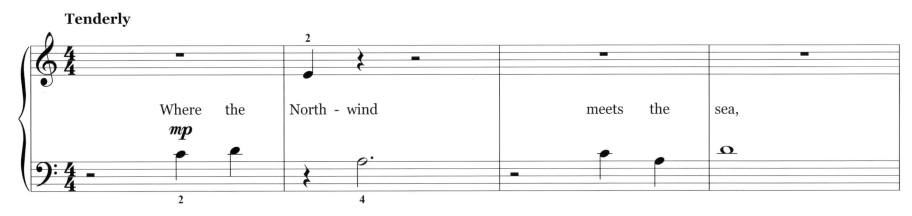

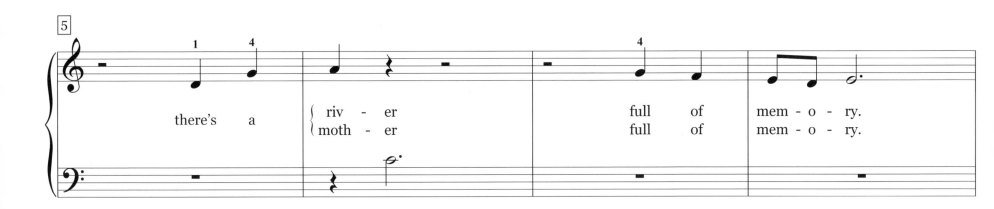

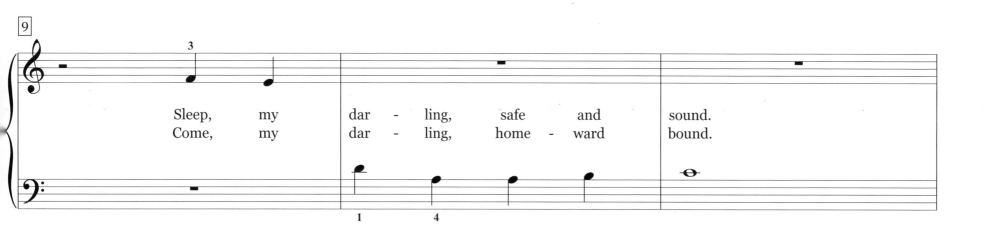

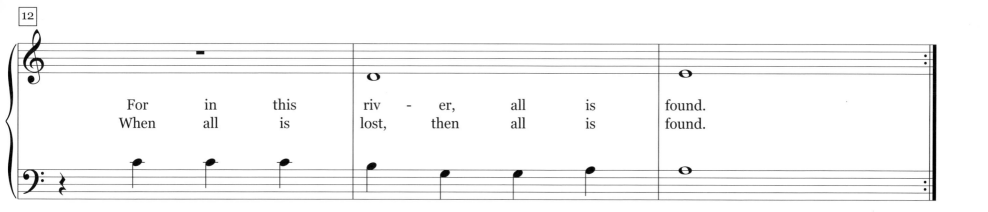

Havana

Words and Music by Camila Cabello, Louis Bell,
Pharrell Williams, Adam Feeney, Ali Tamposi,
Jeffery Lamar Williams, Brian Lee, Andrew Wotman,
Brittany Hazzard and Kaan Gunesberk

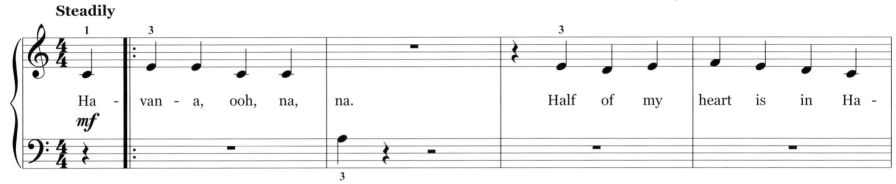

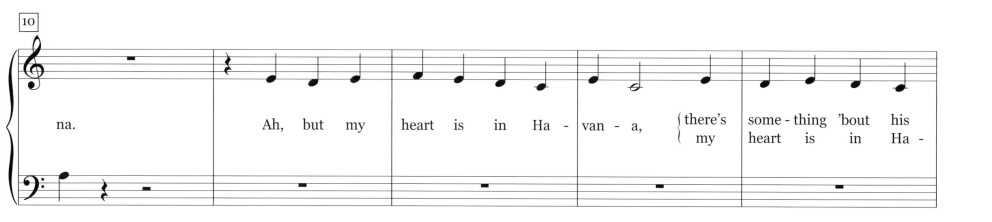

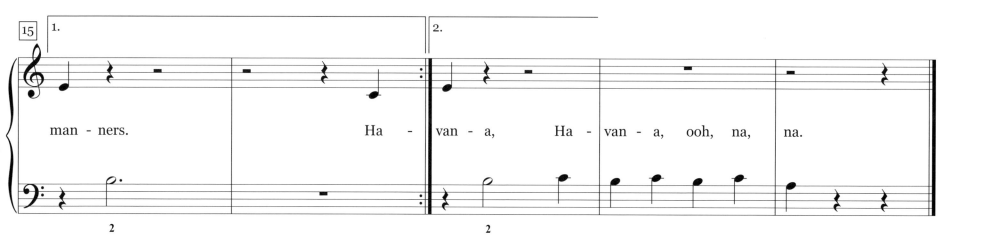

Count on Me

Words and Music by Bruno Mars,
Ari Levine and Philip Lawrence

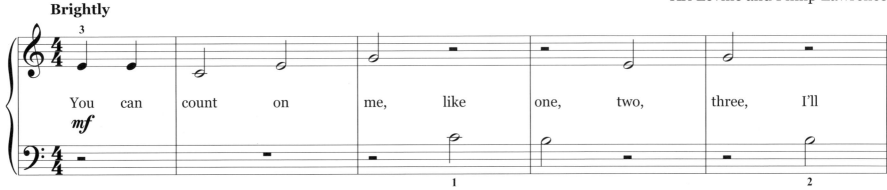

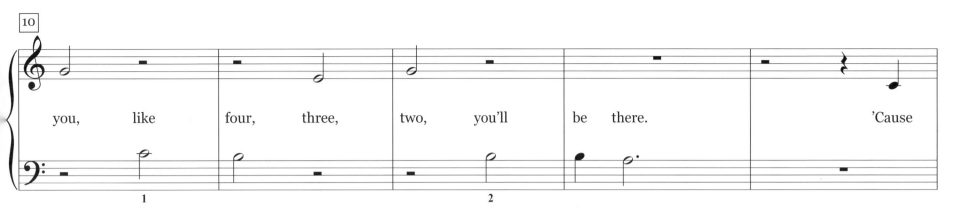

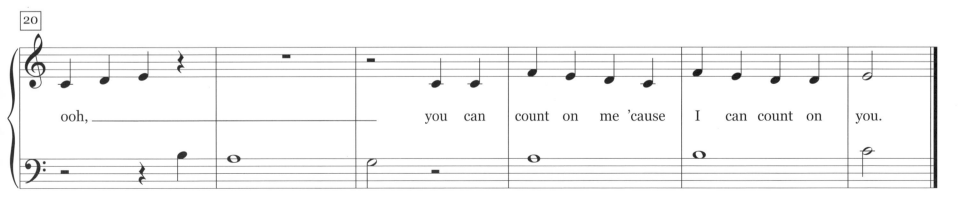

Shallow

from A STAR IS BORN

Words and Music by Stefani Germanotta,
Mark Ronson, Andrew Wyatt
and Anthony Rossomando

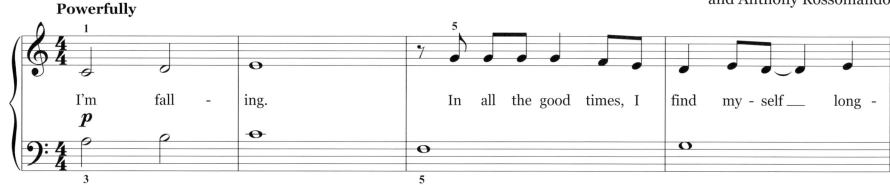

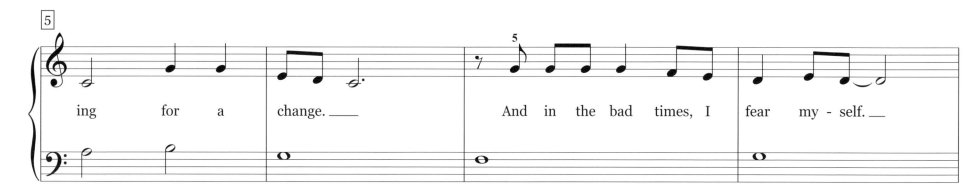

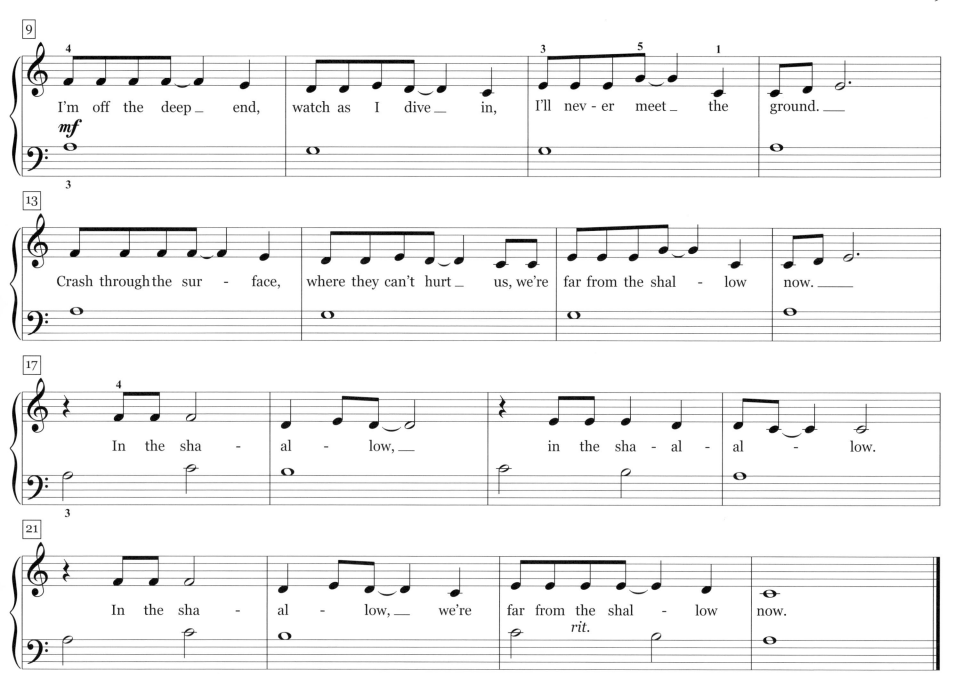

Old Town Road
(I Got the Horses in the Back)

Words and Music by Trent Reznor,
Atticus Ross, Kiowa Roukema
and Montero Lamar Hill

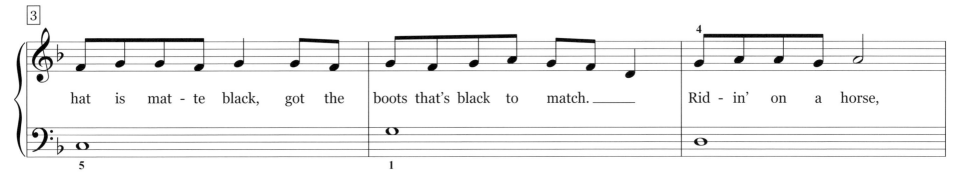

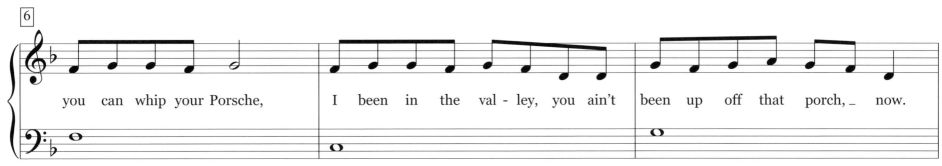

Sign of the Times

Words and Music by Harry Styles,
Jeff Bhasker, Mitch Rowland, Ryan Nasci,
Alex Salibian and Tyler Johnson

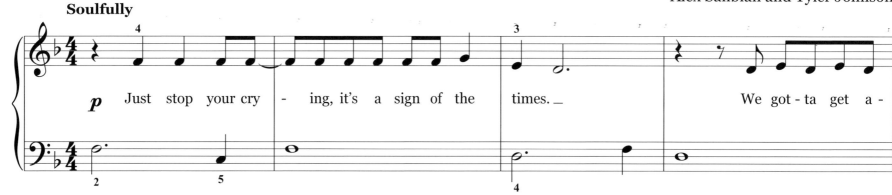

Dynamite

Words and Music by Taio Cruz,
Lukasz Gottwald, Max Martin,
Benjamin Levin and Bonnie McKee

Get Back Up Again

from TROLLS

Words and Music by Justin Paul
and Benj Pasek

A Thousand Years

from the Summit Entertainment film THE TWILIGHT SAGA: BREAKING DAWN - PART 1

Words and Music by David Hodges
and Christina Perri

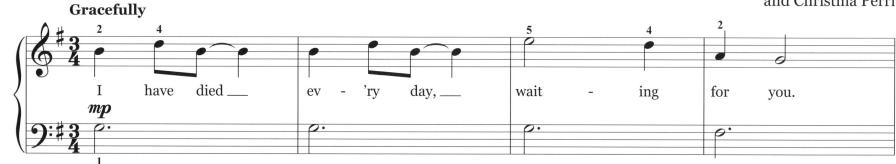

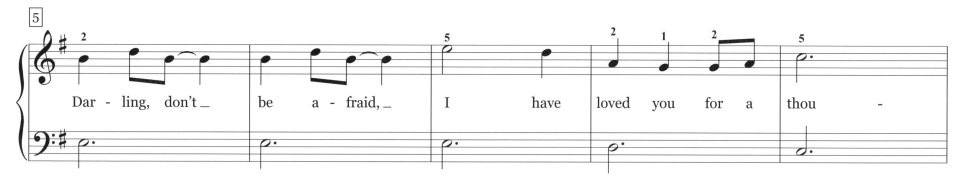

A Million Dreams

from THE GREATEST SHOWMAN

Words and Music by Benj Pasek
and Justin Paul

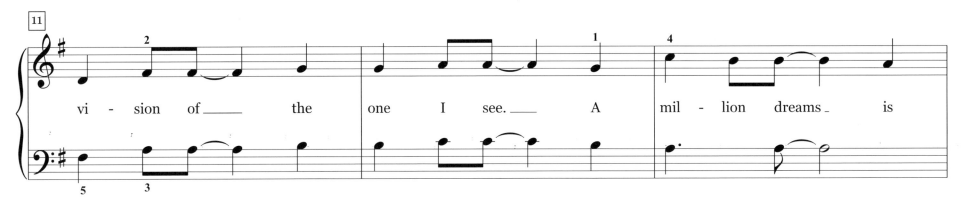

vi - sion of ____ the one I see. ____ A mil - lion dreams ___ is

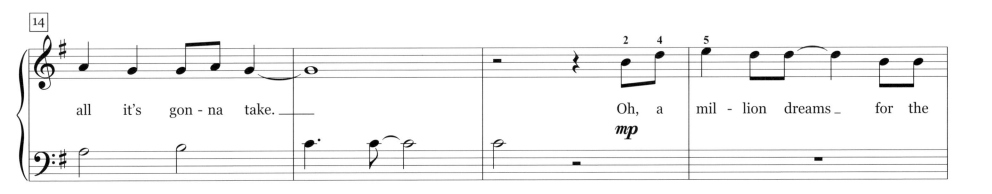

all it's gon - na take. ____ Oh, a mil - lion dreams ___ for the

mp

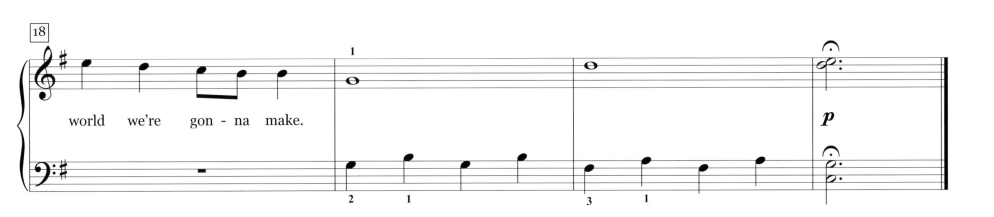

world we're gon - na make.

p

Firework

Words and Music by Katy Perry,
Mikkel Eriksen, Tor Erik Hermansen,
Esther Dean and Sandy Wilhelm

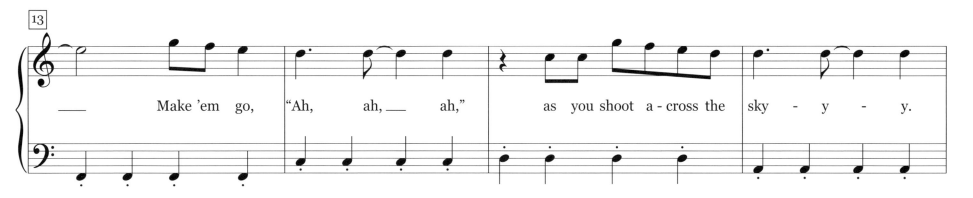

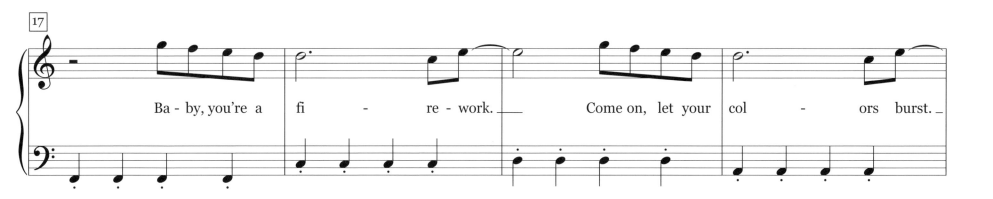

Shotgun

Words and Music by George Barnett,
Joel Laslett Pott and Fred Gibson

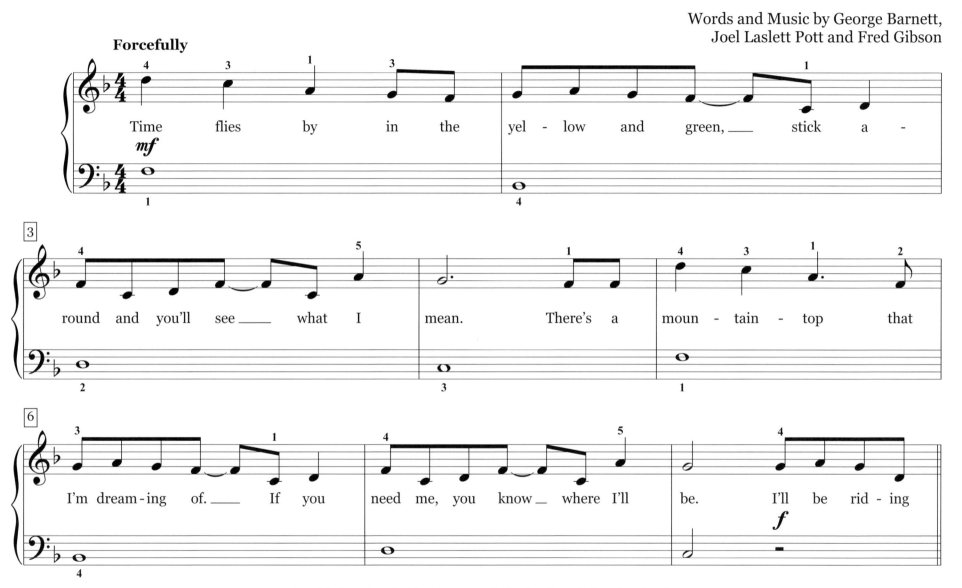

Ocean Eyes

Words and Music by
Finneas O'Connell

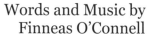

Flowingly

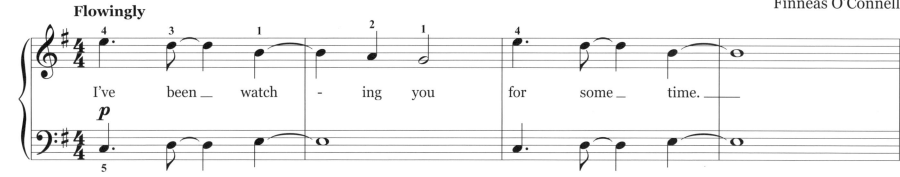

I've been __ watch - ing you for some __ time. __

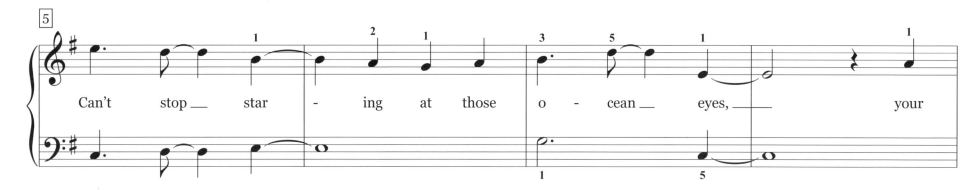

Can't stop __ star - ing at those o - cean __ eyes, __ your

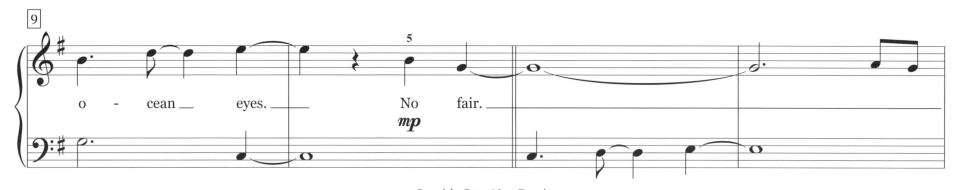

o - cean __ eyes. No fair.

Someone You Loved

Words and Music by Lewis Capaldi,
Benjamin Kohn, Peter Kelleher,
Thomas Barnes and Samuel Roman

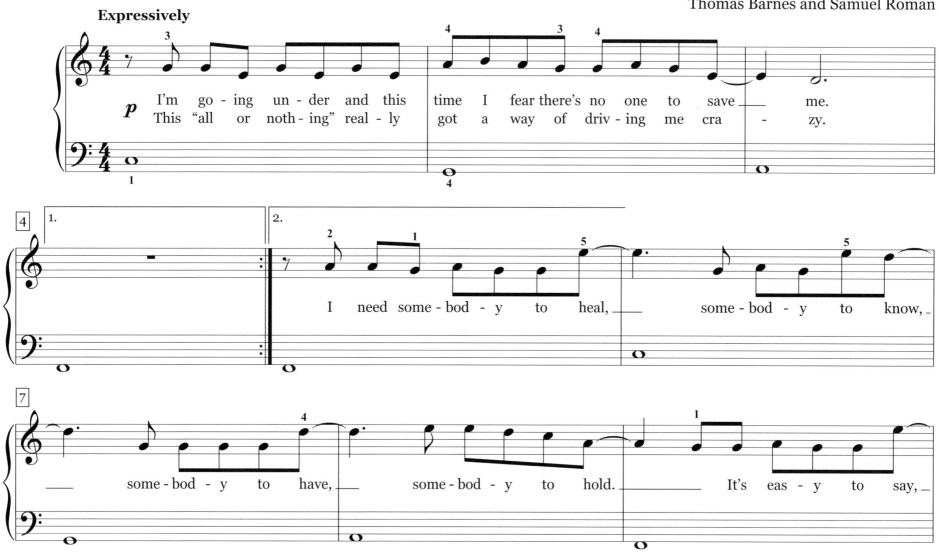

Perfect

Words and Music by
Ed Sheeran

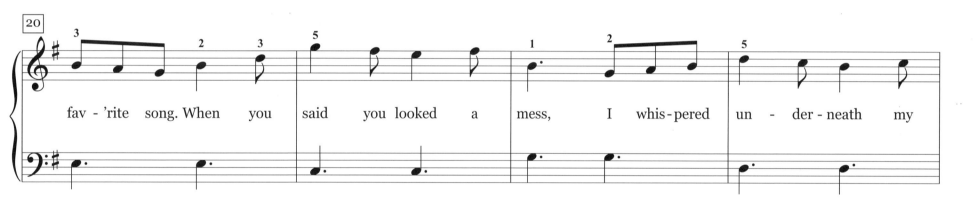

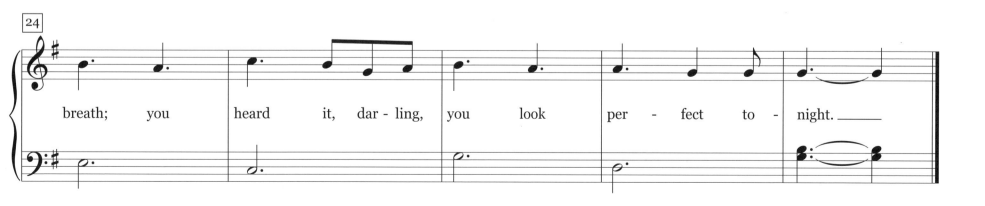

EASIEST PIANO COURSE
Supplementary Songbooks

Fun repertoire books are available as an integral part of **John Thompson's Easiest Piano Course**. Graded to work alongside the course, these pieces are ideal for pupils reaching the end of Part 2. They are invaluable for securing basic technique as well as developing musicality and enjoyment.

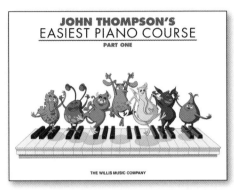

John Thompson's Easiest Piano Course

00414014 Part 1 – Book only $6.99
00414018 Part 2 – Book only $6.99
00414019 Part 3 – Book only $7.99
00414112 Part 4 – Book only $7.99

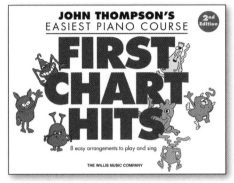

First Beethoven   arr. Hussey

00171709 .... $7.99

First Chart Hits – 2nd Edition

00289560 .... $9.99

First Disney Songs   arr. Miller

00416880 .... $9.99

Also available:

First Children's Songs   arr. Hussey
00282895 ....$7.99

First Classics
00406347 ....$6.99

First Disney Favorites   arr. Hussey
00319587 ....$9.99

First Mozart   arr. Hussey
00171851 ....$7.99

First Nursery Rhymes
00406229 ....$6.99

First Worship Songs   arr. Austin
00416892 ....$8.99

First Jazz Tunes   arr. Baumgartner

00120872 .... $7.99

First Pop Songs   arr. Miller

00416954 .... $8.99

First Showtunes   arr. Hussey

00282907 .... $9.99

EXCLUSIVELY DISTRIBUTED BY

WILLIS MUSIC

HAL•LEONARD®

Prices, contents and availability subject to change without notice.   *Disney Characters and Artwork TM & © 2019 Disney*   View complete songlists and more songbooks on **www.halleonard.com**